RMS
QUEEN M...

OFFICIAL SOUVENIR GUIDE

Compiled by Roger Hardingham

Photographs courtesy of RMS Queen Mary Archives, Carol Cochrane, Roger Hardingham,
J. Christopher Launi, Nicholas Smith and Andy Witherspoon

Published by Boothsprint and Kingfisher Productions ©
Penryn, Cornwall, United Kingdom.

Designed by Jordan Publishing Design Limited, UK   Printed by Boothsprint, UK

Third edition 2017

Your Visit

Welcome to the *R.M.S. Queen Mary!* It is our sincere hope that you enjoy your visit aboard this superb example of the Golden Age of Ocean Travel. In this meticulously produced **Guide Book** the author and publisher have created a wonderful fusion of the *Queen Mary* as she is today as well as how she was in her **Glory Days** in war and peace and in fair weather and foul. The many vintage photographs tell the rich history of her days upon the **North Atlantic Ocean**. The **Guide** also has informative and easy to read deck plans to assist in navigating her many acres of open decks and beautiful interiors. This book will allow the *Queen Mary's* compelling allure and her almost tangible magic to live with you long after your visit.

Commodore Everette Hoard
R.M.S. Queen Mary
Long Beach California

🔱 *A bedroom suite featuring beautiful original fittings combined with modern amenities.*

Welcome aboard the most famous ocean liner in the world. *RMS Queen Mary* has had a long and varied history since she set sail on her maiden voyage from Southampton to New York in May 1936. As you tour the ship you will see many memories from her past. *The Queen Mary's* grand First Class Lounge and Dining Rooms were the largest rooms afloat until the advent of today's cruise ships.

THE QUEEN MARY is today an icon from the past, lovingly preserved in her home of over 40 years – Long Beach, California. You can stay overnight in one of the many staterooms, dine in one of the various restaurants with superb views across the harbor or visit for the day and take the guided tour to find out all the secrets of this 81,000 ton liner.

The hotel features 314 original guest rooms, which include 305 staterooms and 9 full suites. Each stateroom is an original cabin where no two rooms are alike. The size and layout of each room varies. The *Queen Mary's* Long Beach accommodations feature original built-ins and wood paneling – and all rooms include modern amenities, such as iPod, clock radios and flat-panel televisions.

DINE IN ONE OF THE VARIOUS RESTAURANTS WITH SUPERB VIEWS ACROSS THE HARBOR

The elegant Sir Winston's Restaurant at the stern of the ship. This was converted from the engineers' accommodation during the refit in Long Beach.

THE QUEEN MARY offers daily tours where you can explore the ship with an expert guide who will help you discover the history and mystery of the ship. Whether you are interested in art deco design, history, the *Queen Mary's* World War II service or paranormal investigations, our unique tours will give you an in-depth look at the ship's past. There's a lot to see aboard this famous ship so make sure to take a guided *Queen Mary* tour to get the most out of your visit to this Long Beach icon.

Queen Mary and *Queen Elizabeth* passing each other in mid Atlantic during the *Mary*'s final summer in service during 1967. Captain Bill Law of the *Queen Elizabeth* acknowledges the occasion.

The Queen Mary arriving in Long Beach in December 1967.

AFTER 31 YEARS plying across the Atlantic and completing 1001 crossings, the *Queen Mary* is now in sun-blessed California.

Many people ask if the liner is floating. Yes, she rises with the tide each day within a specially-built lagoon for protection. The 1004 foot long waterline and the hull plates below are protected by an electrolytic action device, meaning that her steel plates should never rust.

The *Queen Mary* arrived in Long Beach in December 1967 and immediately went into a dry dock for conversion into a hotel, conference centre, shopping arcade and visitor attraction. It is estimated that around 320 tons of old paint which had accumulated since her launch were stripped from the ship's superstructure in the conversion work.

FACT FILE

The *Queen Mary* was divided into three classes, Cabin, Tourist and Third Class.

The Queen Mary moored inside the lagoon with the Russian 'Scorpion' submarine, now part of the general tour.

TODAY, the *Queen Mary* is constantly being maintained and restored. The lavish Verandah Grill on the sun deck at the stern has been lovingly refurbished. Lifeboats, which are still in place on their davits, have been repaired and many areas of decking have been replaced using teak paneling.

A view along the starboard side showing the restored lifeboats, lagoon and the Pacific Ocean in the far distance. The large air intakes for the engine room are very evident.

FACT FILE

The *Queen Mary* was the first liner to be fitted with fully motorized lifeboats.

The bridge on the Queen Mary was quite spacious and was a hive of activity when the ship was at sea. Full of brass instruments, it was from here that the Captain and crew members would guide the liner during its 1001 crossings of the Atlantic. Telegraph equipment would communicate with the engine room.

The original First Class Lounge is now the Queen's Salon.

The forward end of the Queen's Salon showing the artwork 'Unicorns in Battle' at the far end.

FACT FILE

After World War II 'C' deck was renamed 'R' deck (for restaurant deck). Each of the lower decks was adjusted accordingly and these designations are retained on the ship today.

ONE OF THE most spectacular rooms is the main First Class Lounge. Situated on the Promenade Deck, this lounge was, like the restaurant, in the centre of the liner which gave more comfort to passengers in rough conditions. The lounge had a 'music' theme and this was reflected in artwork which surrounded the room. By day the room was used by First Class passengers to relax, read, or chat in groups. By night the room could be adapted as a ballroom or indeed a cinema. The gesso panel titled 'Unicorns in Battle' by Gilbert Bayes and Alfred Oakley dominates the forward end of the Lounge. Five openings were made in this artwork so that projection equipment could be used to screen the latest sound movies. The room could accommodate 400 people. Three electric fireplaces were sited around the main lounge.

 *The popular Champagne Sunday Brunch is hosted in the Grand Salon, formerly named the First Class Restaurant.*

ON YOUR VISIT to the *Queen Mary* you will see many areas of the ship that were exclusive only to First Class (Cabin) passengers. Situated on 'R' Deck, the First Class restaurant was one of the largest rooms afloat. At 143 feet in length, it was able to accommodate all 815 passengers in this class. Today, this is available for viewing and functions. On Sundays it hosts the famous 'Sunday Brunch', one of the *Mary*'s most popular events. At the forward end of the restaurant is Macdonald Gill's map of the North Atlantic. This became one of the most famous pieces of artwork on the *Queen Mary* and showed two tracks with a crystal model of the ship indicating the position during the voyage.

The First Class Restaurant during the Queen Mary's sea-going days.

CHECK IT OUT...

See if you can spot the crystal model of the *Queen Mary* on the map designed by Macdonald Gill as it used to travel across the splendid artwork.

The Verandah Grill situated on the after deck has returned to the elegant ambiance of the 1930s and 1940s and is now an area for special catered events. Sir Winston's Restaurant, accessed from the starboard side, is the main signature restaurant on board.

Queen Mary alongside Pier J with all the facilities it requires for its modern-day role as an attraction, hotel and a bar and restaurant venue.

A BRIDGE WITH a view. Seen from the main deck, the main bridge and bridge wings had a clear view ahead and to either side of the ship for docking. The forward mast also housed the crow's-nest which was perched some 130 feet above sea level. Access to this was up through the interior of the mast. The crow's-nest had an electric heater and telephone link with the bridge.

THE LAVISH
VERANDAH GRILL ON
THE SUN DECK AT
THE STERN HAS BEEN
LOVINGLY RESTORED.

FACT FILE

Queen Mary snatched the coveted 'Blue Riband' from the liner *Normandie* on her sixth round trip in 1936. She crossed the Atlantic in 4 days 4 hours and 12 minutes.

CHECK IT OUT...

When visiting the *Queen Mary*, you can tour her massive engine room and even view one of her colossal 32 ton, 18½ ft diameter propellers, still attached to the ship. This is viewed from a special platform attached to the hull.

There is now a link to the fore deck and a display of anti-aircraft guns similar to those mounted on the ship during World War II when used as a troopship.

After her maiden voyage, the *Queen Mary* settled into her regular Atlantic crossings from Southampton to New York calling into the French port of Cherbourg. The ship's vulnerability to 'roll' at sea was an uncomfortable problem for passengers. The situation continued until 1958 when stabilizers were fitted.

Photo by J.Christopher Launi

◆ *The Main Hall on the Promenade Deck. This elegant shopping area now boasts a variety of shops selling a wide range of goods and mementoes. The sparkling floor has inlaid art deco designs within it.*

The wide enclosed Promenade Deck is an ideal way of seeing many areas of the great liner. In a pre-maiden voyage cruise in May 1936, British Olympic runner Lord Burghley ran one lap (400 yards) in evening dress around the Promenade Deck in under 60 seconds. ◆

The Travel Bureau is situated on Main Deck. It would have been a hive of activity in earlier times as it was a focal point for passengers wishing further information about their voyage and onward travel arrangements. Today, it is a comfortable seating area for hotel guests.

The Queen Mary was the first ship with a waterline length of over 1000 feet. Her overall length was 1019 feet, just 228 feet shorter than the Empire State Building and 36 feet taller than the Eiffel Tower.

The Quest for Speed

Clydebank, in Glasgow, Scotland on 26th September 1934 with the bow of the *Queen Mary* just visible. His Majesty King George V, within the covered area, makes his speech with his wife and consort, HM Queen Mary behind him on this very dull and wet day by the River Clyde. Her Majesty named the liner after herself, which was until then simply known as John Brown's shipyard Number 534.

THE INSPIRATION for a 1000-foot liner was being considered by the Cunard Steamship Company as early as 1926. Up and until this time, three ships were required to maintain a weekly service across the Atlantic. Cunard's ships *Mauretania*, *Aquitania* and *Berengaria* had been in service for many years and so thoughts were being given to build two larger vessels capable of achieving higher speeds and carrying more passengers on the lucrative route. Speed was calculated to average 33 mph (28.5 knots) by the two new proposed liners and by the late 1920s tests were carried out using 16 foot long models in test tanks simulating all sea and weather conditions the Atlantic could pose. *Queen Mary* would cost in the region of $10,000,000 to complete at 1930s prices.

FACT FILE

2,350 tons of chains were attached to the hull of the liner to hold back the ship as she slid down the slipways and into the River Clyde.

 Tugs maneuver the newly-named Cunard liner after the launching ceremony. At this time, the hull weighed just 35,500 tons. By the time fitting out was complete some 18 months later, the vessel would weigh in at 81,000 tons.

Three huge sirens were fitted to the funnels, one on the middle funnel and two on the forward one. They were 6 feet 7 inches long and were originally operated by steam. They could be heard ten miles away!

CHECK IT OUT...

The builders' plate of John Brown & Co, Clydebank is on display at the forward end of the ship just under the bridge.

CHAIRMAN OF CUNARD, Sir Percy Bates, played down the possibility that the new ships might be built to take the speed record. He stated that Cunard wanted to create a new upmarket service for First Class passengers and take the lead on the North Atlantic from other maritime nations.

FACT FILE

From as early as 1936 all First Class cabins were fitted with telephones. A 640-line switchboard could connect passengers to around the world.

🔹 *The Queen Mary was launched in 1936. She is 1004 ft long on the waterline and displaces 81,237 tonnes as built. The engines produced 160,000 shp giving the ship a top speed of over 30 knots.*

R.M.S.
"QUEEN MARY"

81,237 TONS

PLAN OF
FIRST CLASS
ACCOMMODATION

CUNARD

PROGRESS ON THE first new three-funneled ship was at an advanced stage by 1932 on the slipway at John Brown's shipyard. Many parts of the world were in the grip of the 'Great Depression' and the financial outlook for Britain and America was bleak. The Cunard company was in such a poor state financially it had to halt all work on the liner, putting an estimated 10,000 workers and subcontractors out of work.

FACT FILE

The First Class swimming pool held 110 tons of heated sea water and had to be drained whenever the ship encountered bad weather.

▼ *The Verandah Grill had a theatrical theme to its decor as designed by Doris Zinkeisen. A section of the aft mast penetrates the room on the left. This area was only available to First Class.*

The distinctive light fittings of the Verandah Grill.

CONCERN MOUNTED OVER the rusting hull and superstructure at the shipyard which caused the local Member of Parliament, David Kirkwood, to put pressure on the British government. An agreement was reached whereby Cunard would merge with the struggling White Star Line (owners of the fated *Titanic*) and loans would be given to complete the *Queen Mary*.

R.M.S. "QUEEN MARY"   Friday, August 9, 1957

DINNER

Pineapple Juice

Chilled Grape Fruit

Hors d'Œuvre:
Choux-fleurs, Portugaise   Herrings in Tomato   Anchovy Fillets
Œuf, Rémoulade   Primeurs à l'Huile   Pâte de Foie sur Croûte
Salade Parmentier

Consommé Sarah Bernhardt   Crème Montorgeuil

Grilled Fillets of Whitefish, Mirabeau
Suprême of Halibut, Vin Blanc

Spaghetti au Gratin

Braised Smoked Ox Tongue, Florentine

Roast Ribs and Sirloin of Beef, Horseradish Cream

GRILL: Calf's Liver, Fines-Herbes

French Beans   Squash Mornay
          Boiled and Roast Potatoes

COLD: Roast Leg and Shoulder of Lamb, Mint Sauce
          Spiced Ham

Salads: Chicory   Clover Club   Beetroot
          Cream and Roquefort Dressings

                    Crème Suisse

Ice Cream: Vanilla   Pineapple
    Apples   Pears   Oranges
                    Coffee

Red and White Bordeaux — per Bottle or en Carafe, 7/6; per glass, 1/3
Passengers on Special Diet are especially invited to make known their
          requirements to the Chief Tourist Steward
Speciality Foods for Infants are available on request

TO PRODUCE UP to 40,000 meals per voyage, the *Queen Mary*'s kitchens were a hive of activity. Up-to-date equipment was installed. Most appliances were electrically operated using up to 1,500 kilowatts of power. First Class passengers had breakfast at 8 am, luncheon at 1 pm and dinner at 7.30 pm. Second Class had similar times but two sittings were held. Third Class passengers would have three different sittings at each meal in the 412-seater dining room on C Deck. Menus were printed on board every day.

FACT FILE

On each transatlantic crossing 10,000 meals a day would be supplied, using:

20 tons of fish; 70,000 eggs;
4,000 gallons of milk; 50,000 lbs
of potatoes; 3 tons of butter;
2,000 lbs of cheese.

SECOND CLASS (after 1947 named Cabin Class) catered for up to 787 passengers. Apart from the Dining Room, Second Class passengers had their own Lounge on Main Deck. There was a comfortable atmosphere in this room which also boasted a dance floor area. A supplementary lounge was also available on A Deck. Despite the three classes on board the *Queen Mary*, conditions for all passengers were vastly superior to any other large vessels in service before.

The Lounges would become the social centers of the ship. All three classes had libraries, and in First and Second Class, swimming pools and gymnasiums. Playrooms were available in all classes as were gentlemen's barbers and ladies' hairdressers.

The second Class Dining Room which spanned the width of the liner at the aft end.

FACT FILE

There were 22 elevators on board connecting passengers and crew with 11 decks.

The stylish Observation Bar at the forward end of the ship. It was a popular place for First Class passengers to while away the voyage with a superb view towards the bow.

SECOND CLASS passenger accommodation consisted of 303 staterooms which spanned five decks of the aft end of the ship. The decor was much simpler than First Class but the majority of staterooms had a porthole and views from the ship.

CHILDREN'S PLAYROOMS WERE AVAILABLE IN ALL CLASSES AS WERE GENTLEMENS' BARBERS AND LADIES' HAIRDRESSERS.

Third Class rooms were more basic and situated at the forward end of the *Queen Mary*. This was far less comfortable for passengers as the ship pitched into the rough seas of the North Atlantic on her voyage. There were two and four-berth Third Class rooms to accommodate up to 573 passengers.

CHECK IT OUT...

None of the Second Class or Third Class cabins survive, but a mock-up of one of these cabins is to be seen on C and D Deck.

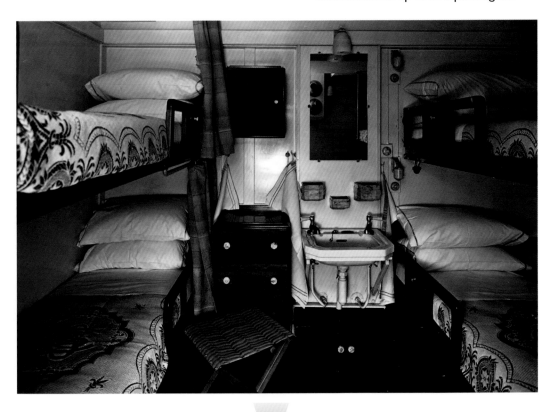

THE THIRD CLASS restaurant was quite basic and without the lavish artwork associated with the other classes. The room was 90 feet long and situated on R Deck just ahead of the forward funnel shaft. The room was just one deck high, at 8 feet 6 inches, compared to three decks high in the First Class Dining Room.

THE ROOM WAS 90 FEET LONG

Passengers in Third Class could relax in the attractive Garden Lounge on Main Deck. It was below the bridge and therefore gave excellent views ahead. Earlier passenger liners tended to copy the interiors of palaces or country houses, but the *Queen Mary* was launched into a more modern era of the 1930s and her designers gave the interior the style of the period. This decor changed after World War II.

An estimated crowd of 250,000 people lined the docks and banks of Southampton Water as the *Queen Mary* left on her maiden voyage on 27th May 1936.

The Queens at War

Just as the Queen Mary settled into her transatlantic career, World War II began in September 1939. For the second time in 25 years world affairs were brought to a virtual standstill and many vessels the size of the *Queen Mary* were requisitioned.

THE MARY WAS in mid Atlantic when news came through that Hitler had invaded Poland. She arrived in New York loaded with passengers on 4th September 1939. Americans were leaving Europe in their thousands and the liner was full on all of her west-bound crossings that summer. *Queen Mary* remained in New York and did not return to Southampton for six years. The ship was berthed in New York for six months and was painted a drab shade of grey in readiness for war service. On 2nd March 1940 the ship was 'called up' and left New York for a secret destination. In fact the ship headed south and was destined for Sydney, Australia.

... DID NOT RETURN TO SOUTHAMPTON FOR SIX YEARS

Meanwhile, Cunard's second liner arrived secretly from her builders on the Clyde. The *Queen Elizabeth*, which was designed to join with the *Queen Mary* on regular Atlantic crossings, now had to enter into war service.

Following some conversion work in Australia, the *Queen Mary* would spend the next six years plying the world's oceans transporting forces to and from war zones, but often returning to Gourock on the river Clyde.

Troops were loaded on board at night and the ship had black-out procedures in place. When at sea, 'zig-zagging' was a common practice to reduce the possibility of a German U-Boat torpedoing the world's largest liner.

FACT FILE

16,683 troops were carried on a single journey during World War II. A record number which remains to this day.

CHECK IT OUT...

Displays about *Queen Mary*'s war service
are situated on C and D Decks. Anti-aircraft
guns similar to those used in World War II
are on display at the forward end.

QUEEN MARY CARRIED over 800,000 troops to many destinations around the world, travelling over 660,000 miles. By April 1945 she was laid-up in New York when it was decided that she was no longer required for active service. The end of the war and VE day (Victory in Europe) came a few weeks later and *Queen Mary*, together with her younger sister, *Queen Elizabeth*, spent the following year repatriating American troops and GI brides until, finally, in September 1946, *Queen Mary* was 'demobilized' and returned to Southampton.

Over the following ten months, the liner was converted back into her peace-time role which had been interrupted six years previously. All the many furnishings and 10,000 pieces of furniture that had been in store in New York, Australia and the UK were brought back to England and eventually returned to the ship.

1500 men from John Brown's shipyard traveled to Southampton, UK and were employed on renovating the ship with local ship-repairers Thornycrofts. The opportunity was taken to convert various areas of the ship including the building of two new Garden Lounges on the Promenade Deck and a cocktail bar. The gymnasium was moved onto the Sun Deck.

Her sister ship, RMS *Queen Elizabeth*, made her commercial maiden voyage to New York as *Queen Mary* returned to Southampton. By July 1947 it was time for the *Mary* to be re-instated to her normal routine on the North Atlantic. The two Queen liners began service on the two-ship, weekly express service across the Atlantic.

FACT FILE

Queen Mary had a tragic collision in 1942 with the British cruiser Curacao off the coast of Ireland. The liner struck the cruiser midships which sank with the loss of 331 lives. *Queen Mary's* bow was severely damaged and was fully repaired in Boston USA.

Mary and the Movies

Famous comedian, Bob Hope (in the center, with l–r, Robert Montgomery, Loretta Young, Alexis Smith, and her husband, Craig Stevens traveled on the Mary often. It was the only way to travel in luxury.

With the *Queen Mary's* fabulous interiors and capacity for giving the very best in accommodation and food, it attracted the most glamorous of lifestyles. The very rich and famous would travel with Cunard's ships which were firmly considered as being 'the only way to cross the Atlantic'. Film stars, politicians and royalty were often be seen on every voyage.

The Duke and Duchess of Windsor regularly shuttled between Europe and the USA. The Duke, as King Edward VIII, abdicated in December 1936 causing a constitutional crisis in Britain.

Prime Minister Winston Churchill regularly traveled on the Queen Mary on official business. His wife, Clementine, seen here, accompanied him many times.

Before air travel was able to offer a more reliable and comfortable form of travel across the Atlantic, Cunard was able to offer high society 'home from home' conditions for their journey to the USA.

Life on the
Ocean Waves

L ife at sea on the *Queen Mary* was very special. The largest liner in the world, until the slightly bigger *Queen Elizabeth* came into operation four years later, would provide passengers with the very best in luxury and style.

"**A City goes to Sea** – Continuously for two months I have been watching all manner of men and women up and down the country, equipping and beautifying this queen of ships. I have seen the fruition of their brains and the finished product of their hands flowing towards the great hull at Clydebank ..."

E. P. Leigh-Bennett 1936

THE QUEEN MARY'S maiden arrival at New York's Pier 90 on Monday 1st June 1936 heralded the completion of 10 years of planning, design, construction and fitting out. Over 30,000 New Yorkers visited the ship following her arrival, such was the publicity and general interest in this huge new liner. America and Britain had been suffering terrible recession and the *Mary*'s entry into service 'lifted the cloud' hanging over the nations. Captain Sir Edgar Britten commanded the first few voyages. The ship took the Blue Riband from the French liner *Normandie* in August 1936 for the fastest ever crossing of the Atlantic.

FACT FILE

Fog interrupted the maiden voyage of the Queen Mary as she approached New York, ending any thought of a record crossing.

The graceful lines of the Queen Mary appear for the first time in New York as the liner docks at Pier 90 following her maiden voyage in 1936.

The elegance of the First Class Main Lounge is seen here with sumptuous furnishings, artwork and even a fireplace. Very much a traditional British setting.

The Long Gallery which was once on the port side of the ship overlooking the Promenade Deck. This room was well known for its comfortable surroundings and elegant lighting.

APART FROM THE traditional deck games, sports facilities were extensive on board the ship and available to all three classes. The First Class gymnasium was located on the port side of the Sun Deck close to the middle funnel. Rowing machines, exercise cycles, punch bags and horse riding machines gave the passengers ample facilities for exercise. However, if this was all too arduous, four laps of the Promenade Deck amounted to one mile!

FACT FILE

John Dempsey was employed in the Turkish Bath and massage area on board from the late 1930s and would meet such stars as David Niven, HG Wells, Bing Crosby, Noel Coward and countless others would go through 'his hands'.

THE FIRST CLASS Swimming Pool was a great draw for passengers with its location on D deck. 60 feet in length and 42 feet wide, the pool was finished in small green glazed briquettes. Indirect lighting lit the pool area as no natural light was available and the whole room was one of the finest locations on the liner. With the North Atlantic being rough much of the year, the pool was often drained of its water for safety reasons.

The First Class Swimming Pool is no longer available for use but is a feature of the guided tour. The Second Class pool was located at the stern of the ship on F Deck but was removed in the conversion of the *Mary* on arrival at Long Beach in 1967.

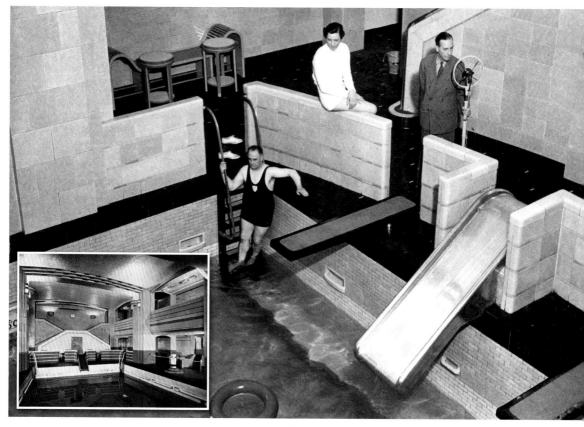

Art on the Queen Mary

The *Queen Mary* was full of art. Artists and artisans were commissioned by Cunard to style and decorate the interiors of the largest, fastest and grandest ship on the North Atlantic. Her twenty-five public rooms were adorned with the best of British decorative arts and finished with veneers from rare woods drawn from all of His Majesty's colonies.

Painting by Anna Zinkeisen in the Ballroom on Promenade Deck

The Shipbuilder and Marine Engine-Builder magazine from 1936:

"The modern influence undoubtedly exists, but rampant modernity has been studiously and successfully avoided. The result is everywhere delightful, the beautifully balanced decorations and appointments combining to produce an atmosphere of rich, although unobtrusive, luxury which pervades the whole vessel."

All the art for the *Queen Mary's* public rooms was designed jointly under the direction of architects Benjamin Wistar Morris and Arthur J. Davis. Morris was an American who had designed the Cunard building in New York and brought his talent to woo the American passenger. Davis was British and trained at the same school of art in Paris that Morris had attended. He would be responsible for selecting the firms carrying out the furnishings which would be in line with Cunard's conservative attitude of the time.

A wood carving by Bainbridge Copnall from the First Class Restaurant.

A detailed decorative scene from a First Class Stateroom.

Painting over the fireplace in the First Class Drawing Room by Kenneth Shoesmith.

🦋 *Macdonald Gill's decorative map of the North Atlantic. This magnificent map is located in the First Class Restaurant on R Deck. An electrically lit crystal model of the Queen Mary traveled across the map as the ship progressed between the New and Old worlds.*

EVERY ROOM dedicated to First Class, mostly located on the Promenade Deck, was full of art: from the Observation Bar at the forward end, to the First Class Lounge,

Restaurant, Ballroom, Smoking Room,
Verandah Grill and Drawing Room.
These rooms were also laden with
specially designed textiles and fabrics,
carpets and upholsteries.

FACT FILE

Over 30 artists were commissioned to produce the
hundreds of items of artwork and furnishings for
Queen Mary.

The personal standard of HM Queen Mary presented to RMS Queen Mary.

One of three mural carvings by John Skeaping from the Starboard Gallery on Promenade Deck.

'The Sea' by Edward Wadsworth in the First Class Smoking Room.

One of Doris Zinkeisen's decorative paintings in the Verandah Grill on Sun Deck.

Marble plaque by Lady Hilton Young of HM Queen Mary located on the staircase facing the main shopping area.

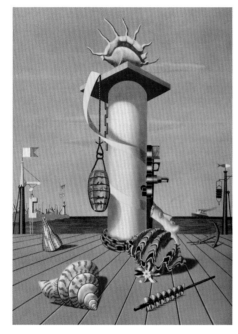

An illuminated glass panel by Charles Cameron Baillie from the Second Class Swimming Pool.

A carved screen in limewood by James Woodford in the First Class Smoking Room.

A
New Life
in California

After World War II, RMS *Queen Mary* sailed through the 1950s and early 1960s very successfully for its owners. During the summer months both the Queens were full to capacity but less so in winter. The ship tended to roll a great deal in heavy seas. Because of this stabilizers were fitted in 1958 which helped reduce the problem.

Queen Mary departs from New York for the very last time in September 1967.

THE BIGGEST THREAT to the two Cunarders was the increase in air travel from Europe to America. By the early 1960s the *Queen Mary* was running only one quarter full and still with a full complement of crew. Decisions as to the economics of keeping the liner in service had to be made and Cunard opted to try and adapt *Queen Mary* for cruises rather than solely on the North Atlantic run. Her first cruise was to Las Palmas in 1963 followed by other cruises to the Bahamas and the Mediterranean. Alterations were made to some of the main rooms to reflect the new role. The Second Class Lounge was decorated as the Flamenco Room and for the first time, the Observation Bar was given over to Second or Tourist classes.

These measures did little to make the ship more profitable and with 4,000,000 passengers opting for air travel compared to 650,000 by sea in 1965, the writing was on the wall for both the big Cunard vessels.

Chairman of Cunard, Sir Basil Smallpiece wrote in May 1967,

" *It is a matter of great regret to the Company and to me personally, as it will be to friends throughout the world, that these two fine ships, the Queen Mary and Queen Elizabeth, must shortly come to the end of their working lives.* "

Queen Mary was put up for sale in a bidding process and on 24th July 1967 the City of Long Beach was the successful bidder for the ship at $3,450,000. The *Queen Mary* would make her final trip from Southampton to Long Beach, full of passengers, on 'The Last Great Cruise' leaving Southampton on 31st October 1967. The voyage would take the liner to Lisbon, Las Palmas, across to Rio de Janeiro, round Cape Horn for an arrival in California on 9th December. The *Queen Mary* then entered four years of dry-docking and conversion into a hotel, series of restaurants and tourist attractions. After 1001 crossings of the Atlantic, and six years of war service, the grand old lady was beginning a new life in the sunshine state for all to enjoy.

CHECK IT OUT...

Captain John Treasure Jones commanded the final voyage from Southampton to Long Beach. Several old red London buses and telephone boxes were strapped to the deck for the passage to America. Many passengers boarded the buses as the ship passed round Cape Horn to say they had traveled round by a London bus!

The *Queen Mary* ends her career at sea on 9th December 1967 accompanied by hundreds of boats in Long Beach harbor.

The historic rendezvous of the *Queen Mary* and *Queen Mary 2* on 23rd February 2006. The picture is reproduced by kind permission of Long Beach City photographer, Andy Witherspoon. His late father, Tom, was the official City photographer on "The Last Great Cruise" in 1967 from Southampton to Long Beach.

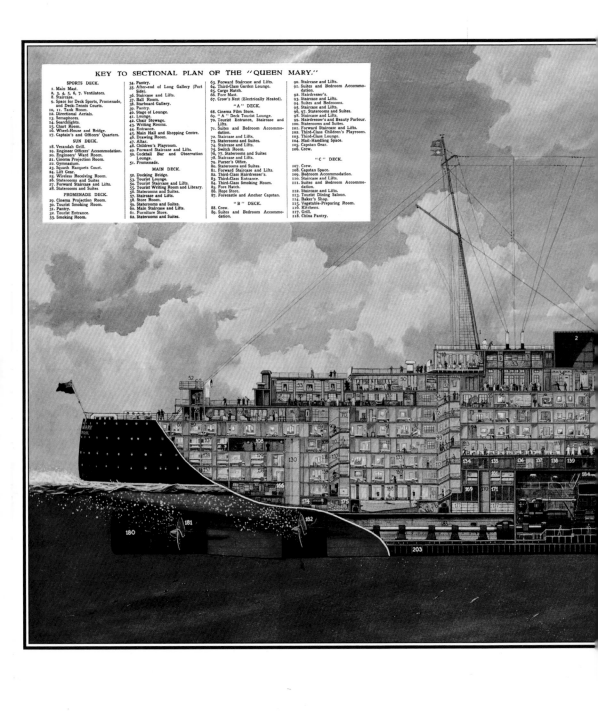

KEY TO SECTIONAL PLAN OF THE "QUEEN MARY."

SPORTS DECK.
1. Main Mast.
2, 3, 4, 5, 6, 7. Ventilators.
8. Staircase.
9. Space for Deck Sports, Promenade, and Deck-Tennis Courts.
10, 11. Tank Room.
12. Directional Aerials.
13. Semaphores.
14. Searchlights.
15. Chart Room.
16. Wheel-House and Bridge.
17. Captain's and Officers' Quarters.

SUN DECK.
18. Verandah Grill.
19. Engineer Officers' Accommodation.
20. Engineers' Ward Room.
21. Cinema Projection Room.
22. Gymnasium.
23. Squash Racquets Court.
24. Lift Gear.
25. Wireless Receiving Room.
26. Staterooms and Suites.
27. Forward Staircase and Lifts.
28. Staterooms and Suites.

PROMENADE DECK.
29. Cinema Projection Room.
30. Tourist Smoking Room.
31. Pantry.
32. Tourist Entrance.
33. Smoking Room.
34. Pantry.
35. After-end of Long Gallery (Port Side).
36. Staircase and Lifts.
37. Ball Room.
38. Starboard Gallery.
39. Pantry.
40. Stage of Lounge.
41. Lounge.
42. Chair Stowage.
43. Writing Rooms.
44. Entrance.
45. Main Hall and Shopping Centre.
46. Drawing Room.
47. Altar.
48. Children's Playroom.
49. Forward Staircase and Lifts.
50. Cocktail Bar and Observation Lounge.
51. Promenade.

MAIN DECK.
52. Docking Bridge.
53. Tourist Lounge.
54. Tourist Staircase and Lifts.
55. Tourist Writing Room and Library.
56. Staterooms and Suites.
57. Staircase and Lifts.
58. Store Room.
59. Staterooms and Suites.
60. Main Staircase and Lifts.
61. Furniture Store.
62. Staterooms and Suites.
63. Forward Staircase and Lifts.
64. Third-Class Garden Lounge.
65. Cargo Hatch.
66. Fore Mast.
67. Crow's Nest (Electrically Heated).

"A" DECK.
68. Cinema Film Store.
69. "A" Deck Tourist Lounge.
70. Tourist Entrance, Staircase and Lifts.
71. Suites and Bedroom Accommodation.
72. Staircase and Lifts.
73. Staterooms and Suites.
74. Staircase and Lifts.
75. Switch Room.
76, 77. Staterooms and Suites.
78. Staircase and Lifts.
79. Purser's Office.
80. Staterooms and Suites.
81. Forward Staircase and Lifts.
82. Third-Class Hairdresser's.
84. Third-Class Smoking Room.
85. Fore Hatch.
86. Rope Store.
87. Forecastle and Anchor Capstan.

"B" DECK.
88. Crew.
89. Suites and Bedroom Accommodation.
90. Staircase and Lifts.
91. Suites and Bedroom Accommodation.
92. Hairdresser's.
93. Staircase and Lifts.
94. Suites and Bedrooms.
95. Staircase and Lifts.
96, 97. Staterooms and Suites.
98. Staircase and Lifts.
99. Hairdresser's and Beauty Parlour.
100. Staterooms and Suites.
101. Forward Staircase and Lifts.
102. Third-Class Children's Playroom.
103. Third-Class Lounge.
104. Mail-Handling Space.
105. Capstan Gear.
106. Crew.

"C" DECK.
107. Crew.
108. Capstan Space.
109. Bedroom Accommodation.
110. Staircase and Lifts.
111. Suites and Bedroom Accommodation.
112. Staircase and Lifts.
113. Tourist Dining Saloon.
114. Baker's Shop.
115. Vegetable-Preparing Room.
116. Kitchens.
117. Grill.
118. China Pantry.

Deck plans of the *Queen Mary*

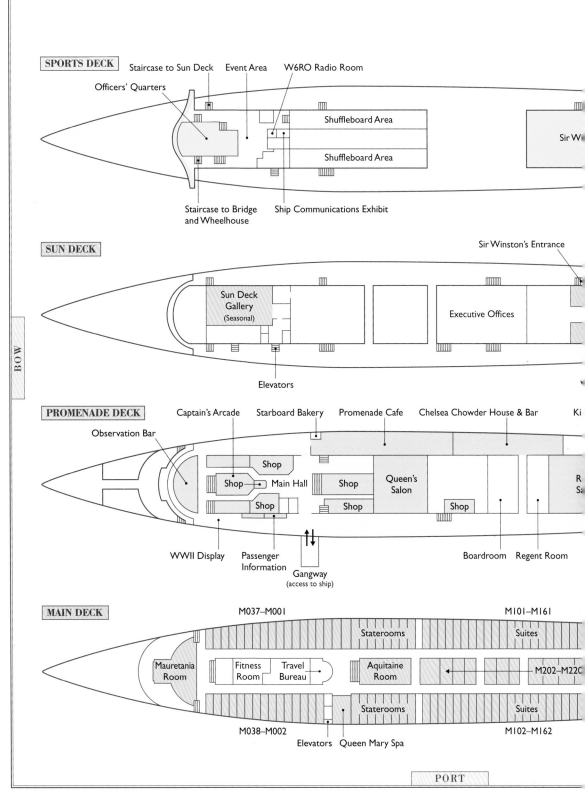

SPORTS DECK

Officers' Quarters

Staircase to Sun Deck Event Area W6RO Radio Room

Shuffleboard Area

Shuffleboard Area

Sir W

Staircase to Bridge and Wheelhouse Ship Communications Exhibit

SUN DECK

Sir Winston's Entrance

Sun Deck Gallery (Seasonal)

Executive Offices

Elevators

PROMENADE DECK

Captain's Arcade Starboard Bakery Promenade Cafe Chelsea Chowder House & Bar Ki

Observation Bar

Shop

Shop Main Hall

Shop

Shop

Queen's Salon

R Sa

Shop

Shop

Shop

WWII Display Passenger Information Boardroom Regent Room

Gangway (access to ship)

MAIN DECK

M037–M001

M101–M161

Staterooms

Suites

Mauretania Room

Fitness Room

Travel Bureau

Aquitaine Room

M202–M220

Staterooms

Suites

M038–M002

M102–M162

Elevators Queen Mary Spa

BOW

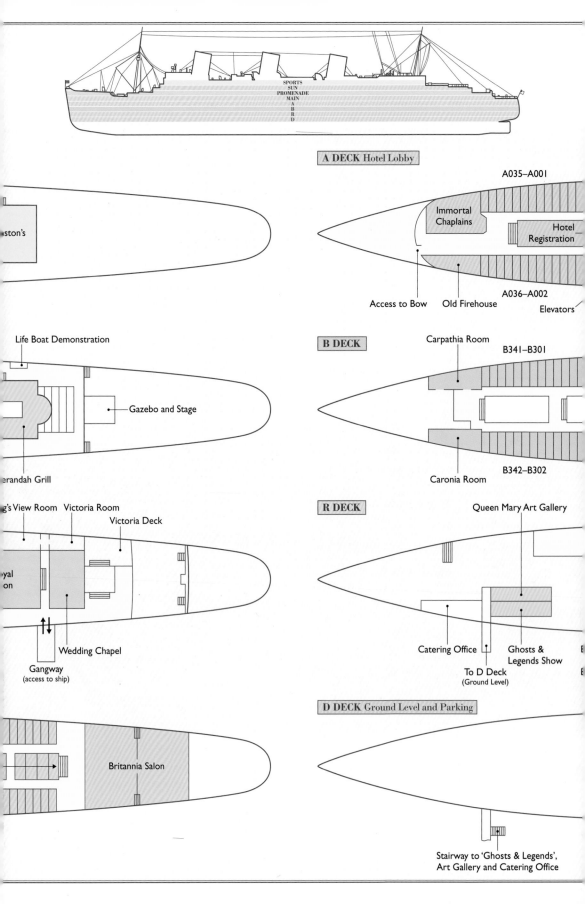

SPORTS
SUN
PROMENADE
MAIN
A
B
R
D

A DECK Hotel Lobby

A035–A001

ston's

Immortal
Chaplains

Hotel
Registration

Access to Bow   Old Firehouse

A036–A002

Elevators

Life Boat Demonstration

B DECK

Carpathia Room

B341–B301

Gazebo and Stage

erandah Grill

Caronia Room

B342–B302

g's View Room   Victoria Room

Victoria Deck

R DECK

Queen Mary Art Gallery

yal
on

Catering Office

Ghosts &
Legends Show

Wedding Chapel

To D Deck
(Ground Level)

Gangway
(access to ship)

D DECK Ground Level and Parking

Britannia Salon

Stairway to 'Ghosts & Legends',
Art Gallery and Catering Office